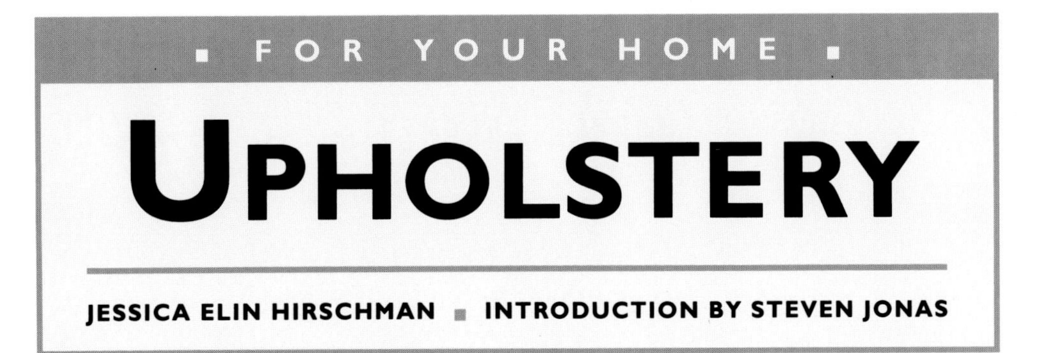

FOR YOUR HOME

# UPHOLSTERY

JESSICA ELIN HIRSCHMAN ■ INTRODUCTION BY STEVEN JONAS

# Dedication

For my brother, Gregory Elin, who finds colour, texture, and pattern in everything...and has taught me to do the same.

# Acknowledgements

I would like to extend my sincerest appreciation to the inspired designers and artists whose work graces these pages and whose assistance in compiling this book was invaluable; the dedicated staff of the Michael Friedman Publishing Group, particularly newcomer Colleen Branigan; and Steven Jonas, without whose insight, talent, and experience this book would not have been possible.

**A FRIEDMAN GROUP BOOK**

Published 1993 by Merehurst Limited
Ferry House, 51/57 Lacy Road
Putney, London SW15 1PR

By arrangement with Michael Friedman Publishing Group, Inc.



ISBN 1 85391 284 0



A catalogue record for this book is available from the British Library.

*FOR YOUR HOME: UPHOLSTERY*
was prepared and produced by
Michael Friedman Publishing Group, Inc.
15 West 26th Street
New York, New York 10010

Editor: Dana Rosen
Designer: Lynne Yeamans
Art Director: Jeff Batzli
Photography Editors: Christopher C. Bain and Colleen Branigan
Production Director: Karen Matsu Greenberg

Colour separations by Bright Arts (Singapore) Pte. Ltd.
Printed and bound in Hong Kong by Leefung-Asco Printers Ltd.

# Table of Contents

ARMISTEAD MAUPIN BABYCAKES

# INTRODUCTION

Next to the architectural design of a space, nothing sets the mood of a room or defines personal style more than upholstered furniture. But unlike architecture, with its rigid, permanent lines, upholstery makes a personal connection, offering a special type of comfort and inviting us to enjoy it through physical touch.

For centuries, all furniture, especially upholstered pieces, was designed to meet the tastes and needs of a society's elite members — the royalty, the nobility, and the very wealthy. Its unique importance to these select individuals is evident in historical records. For example, upholsterers were the only craftspeople allowed to pass through the front entrance to the grand establishments of both Russian and French nobility. Often, the budgets that were allotted for elaborate upholstered furniture exceeded those for all other household goods, including art and clothing.

As with other material objects, furniture has been a symbol of power and prestige throughout history. Upholstery, which demands a variety of materials and a range of skills to execute properly, was for centuries considered a status symbol. It wasn't until a middle class developed in Western society around the 1500s that a great number of people began to acquire upholstered furniture and to provide

**Left:** IN A SMALL SUNROOM, A WARM PALETTE SOOTHES AND UNIFIES THE INTENTIONALLY OVERDONE COLLECTION OF FABRICS, PATTERN, TEXTURE, AND DETAIL. THE SMALL SCALE OF THE SOFA'S WOVEN SILK DIAMOND MOTIF CONTRASTS WITH THE LARGER PATTERN OF THE SURROUNDING EMPIRE WALLPAPER. **Above:** SOLID FABRICS THE COLORS OF PEACHES, PLUMS, AND BLUEBERRIES REVIVE A BLAND BEIGE LIVING ROOM COUCH RESTYLED FOR THE FAMILY ROOM. AN ABSTRACT CHINTZ WITH STRIPED BLACK AND WHITE FRENCH PIPING ROUND OUT THE KALEIDOSCOPE OF COLOR AND PATTERN.

themselves with a higher level of comfort.

The history of a society's furniture is closely related to its cultural sophistication. While beds, chairs, and sofas were originally valued for their functionality, in many societies furniture acquired more ornamentation and its decorative aspect was emphasized. Ancient Egypt was the first civilization known to use upholstery. The dry climate of the region helped to preserve the everyday objects the Egyptians sealed in their tombs, giving us a close-up look at beds, chairs, and sofas used thousands of years ago. While the common people usually owned only simple items like three-legged stools, members of the king's palace, landowners, and the nobility enjoyed elaborate pieces of furniture, especially beds. Egyptian beds boasted ornate legs of carved wood, which were usually shaped like lions. Mattresses were supported on woven leather latticework. Handsome fabrics were carefully sewn onto cushions to enhance beds and chairs.

In Roman society, as in Egypt, upholstered furniture was reserved for the elite, who reclined on sofas for reading, sleeping, drinking, and even dining. The Greeks were the first in the Western world to use silk to lavishly decorate their upholstered furniture — the ancestors of

**Above:** A claret-colored couch is upholstered in a style reminiscent of Victorian England, when bands of hand-worked needlepoint decorated seat and back cushions covered in solid colors. Other Victorian-inspired details include deep bullion fringe, a tufted ottoman with lined box pleats, and art hung from taffeta bows. The more contemporary scalloped skirt style used on the pair of Napoleon III–inspired upholstered chairs unobtrusively stops the space from becoming a period room.

today's modern chaise lounge and sofa.

Virtually all predecessors of today's most popular furniture styles are rooted in eastern and western Europe, since both the Chinese and Japanese have customarily slept and sat on pillows and floor mats. Oriental influences appear in the shape of a leg or in carved details, but upholstery itself developed in Italy, England, France, Spain, Germany, and Russia. While each region had its own style and methods, all made contributions to the development of upholstery. The Germans, for instance, were the first to use hand-stitched horsehair in upholstery. Prior to the introduction of horsehair, which is still used today since it holds its shape without loss of comfort, the English used dried sea moss. The French added finesse by introducing tufting, fringes, and pleats.

Italian artisans designed the first important furniture of the Renaissance. Chests, which were prominent during the Middle Ages, now had backrests and arms added to them. The *cassapanca*, a chest for storing clothing, was used both as a bench and as a chest. Revival of interest in the classical cultures resulted in many rich Italian merchants filling their newly built palaces with upholstered pieces resembling those used by the Greeks. By the early 1600s, people of all classes considered the quality of a household's uphol-

**Above:** In this family room, the upholstery colors, textures, and patterns strike an attractive balance between a rejuvenating springlike sunroom and a warm, cozy winter nest. The careful placement of throw pillows visually joins together the many fabrics and moods.

stery to be an indicator of social rank. Large "state beds" lavishly decorated with silk and velvet fabrics were now being placed not only in bedrooms, but in the main rooms of palaces and large houses.

In the late 1600s, King Louis XIV of France intensified furniture's role as a status symbol. He was convinced that decorative arts, especially fine upholstered furniture, would boost his political importance by glorifying his position as king. Expert artisans were commissioned to convert Versailles from a large hunting lodge into a grand palace. They developed a distinctly French style of upholstery that emphasized details such as pleats, trims, and tufting. This style was later imitated in palaces throughout Europe.

While upholstered pieces have changed in form throughout the ages — ranging from fussy French styles to the overstuffed English chairs and sofas of the Victorian and Edwardian periods — the proper construction of handmade upholstery has remained constant. The basic structure of an upholstered piece begins with the frame. High-quality pieces use only kiln-dried zero-defect woods, which are free of knots. In the United States, the preferred wood is usually maple, while European craftspeople typically use beechwood. All joints are double-dowelled with screwed corner blocks, which reinforces the stability of the frame. This method prevents a weak or shifting infrastructure.

**Above:** LINEN, BLENDED WITH MOHAIR TO MINIMIZE WRINKLING AND ENHANCE SOFTNESS, COVERS A SOFA AND CHAIR INCORPORATED INTO 1930S SURROUNDINGS. PILLOWS COVERED IN SILK FAUX ZEBRA AND A TWO-COLOR LEATHER OTTOMAN ADD BITS OF COLOR IN AN APARTMENT SHOWCASING ORIGINAL ARTWORK.

Next, coil springs are strategically tacked on. Each one is tied twelve times in the seat of a chair or ottoman to assure that both the correct form and the right feel are achieved. Each style demands a different configuration of springs, but generally the larger coils are laced toward the back of a seat to accommodate the bulk of a person's weight. The series of springs on the seat gradually becomes thinner toward the front edge of a chair or sofa. The springs on the back of a chair or sofa are tied eight times (the fewer times a coil is tied, the less resistance it offers), and graduate from thicker to thinner coils from the bottom up. Curled horsehair is then stitched to burlap, and another burlap layer is stitched to the first layer and to the springs. About twenty pounds (9kg) of horsehair is used in a typical high-grade upholstered chair; this horsehair, along with the burlap, creates the shape and foundation of a piece. This foundation is then covered with glazed cotton fabric, and blanketlike down pads are layered over the cotton.

Depending on one's budget and personal preference, the chair or sofa's cushions can be pure white goose down, which is the most costly and offers the softest, plushest look and feel, or a down and feather combination, which is priced depending upon the ratio of down to feathers. Those who prefer a firmer and/or less expensive piece can request down with a foam core.

**Above:** Cotton and linen velvet, cotton velour, and leather and eelskin upholstery bring textural dimension to an understated palette of ecru and silvery gray. Woven polka dot pillows accent the hand-woven linen rug.

Foam core also requires less maintenance, since all down cushions need some fluffing and shaping after use. A typical well-crafted upholstered armchair requires about twelve pounds (5.5kg) of down. Once the down cushions are in place, a white muslin is hand-stitched over them. With this step, the piece is ready for the cutting, placing, and stitching of the fabric. The cords, trim, pleats, and other details constitute the final phase of construction.

As with many hand-crafted arts, only a handful of shops remain that are dedicated to executing quality upholstered furniture the Old World way. An increasing number of upholstered pieces today are finished in high-quality fabrics but borrow the manufacturing practices of machine-made operations. By carefully inspecting an upholstered piece and asking some specific questions, a consumer can better understand the quality of the piece he or she is buying. The better the construction, the longer the life of the furniture and the more likely it can someday be reupholstered, an obviously less expensive alternative to purchasing a replacement piece.

One aspect to consider before buying is the inner spring construction. A quality piece of furniture uses a spring-edge seat, which significantly helps prevent the

**Above:** A vivid yellow wool with sculptured pin dots announces a small 1930s chair found in a Paris flea market. The recovered fabric buttons and self welting are historically appropriate. Navy blue canvas now covers a 1927 Bauhaus-inspired design originally upholstered in khaki. Together, the primary colors impart a relaxed quality to the room.

front edge of the seat from breaking down. It also makes for a softer, more comfortable edge than a wooden one. The springs in a better-made piece are tacked and tied individually rather than in groups or units. Another way to ensure that a piece is well-made is to feel the corners and edges in order to determine the quality of the stuffing. You should not be able to feel the wooden frame through the fabric. In addition, the legs should be an integral part of the frame; legs that have been added on can weaken a piece, make it unstable, and even break off. Another indication of high quality is webbing and springs that are sewn together. And the amount of down, feather, or foam used in the cushions will determine how well the piece will hold up — the more man-made fibers, such as foam, that are used, the more rapidly the cushions will break down.

Top-quality upholstered pieces traditionally are kept for generations and are passed down as heirlooms from one family member to another. A hand-crafted chair or sofa not only will retain its value through the years, but like Dad's favorite well-worn armchair, will eventually assume the status of a comforting, loyal, and irreplaceable old friend.

**Above:** COLOR, PATTERN, AND FORM COME TOGETHER IN THE CANDY CANE CHAIR, AN ORIGINAL DESIGN WHIMSICALLY UPHOLSTERED IN A SPUNKY HOT PINK AND YELLOW SILK THAT WAS WOVEN SPECIFICALLY FOR THIS STANDOUT CHAIR. THE CHAIR'S BOLD STRIPES ACCENTUATE ITS HIGH SCROLLED BACK AND VOLUPTUOUSLY CURVED SEAT CUSHION; A MATCHING SILK BULLION FRINGE DANGLES DECORATIVELY ABOVE GILDED LEGS.

**Left:** A creamy cotton damask imparts antique charm to a modern-day overstuffed sofa. The tone-on-tone pattern was chosen so as not to overshadow the eighteenth-century side chairs, which are covered in a cotton chintz copied from a period silk taffeta. The use of a single print in tandem with a solid-colored fabric helps calm this well-accessorized conversation area.

**Above:** A small sofa is covered in the same quail-pattern cotton chintz used elsewhere in this room. The skirt features pleats and a richly tasseled fringe. **Left:** A closer look at the opulent cream-colored sofa featured at far left reveals the clever conversion of a tasseled drapery tieback into a distinct finishing touch. An open braid fashioned from ivory-colored French-style silk cording adorns the dressmaker-style skirt.

**Above:** Drawing on the palette of a museum-quality rug for inspiration, the designer of this living room chose silk brocade for the upholstered armchair; bengaline, a finely woven cotton similar to corduroy, for the antique Italian gilt wood chairs; and linen velvet, because it wears well, for the sofa. Antique clerical vestments discovered at auctions cover the accent pillows. **Right:** A blend of costly and inexpensive fabrics imparts character to furniture without breaking the budget. Here, oversized casual-style pillows are covered in exquisite European silk damasks, and the ottoman features expensive mohair with a formal bullion fringe. By contrast, the sofas are upholstered in an affordable purple cotton damask and a good-quality gold cotton velvet dressed up with contrasting trim and multicolored fringe.

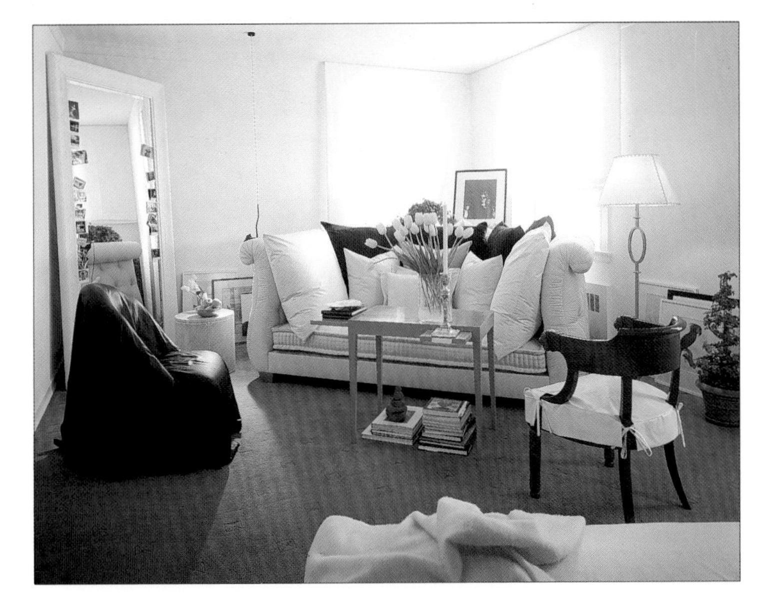

**Left, top:** WASHABLE FABRICS MAKE THE MOST PRACTICAL SLIPCOVERS, PARTICULARLY WHEN THE DESIRED COLOR IS WHITE. IN THIS BEDROOM, A TAILORED COTTON CHINTZ SLIPCOVER GIVES THE BED A SOFT, REFRESHING LOOK. A LOOSELY SLIPCOVERED CHAIR AND A COLLECTION OF INTERNATIONAL FURNISHINGS KEEPS THE ROOM FROM APPEARING TOO COMPOSED.

**Left, bottom:** SIMPLE SLIPCOVERS CREATED FOR THIS ROOM INCLUDE A LEATHER HIDE TUCKED INTO A CHAIR AND A DAINTY PIECE OF COTTON FABRIC TIED TO A SEAT. BOTH TECHNIQUES MAKE REDECORATING A ONE-ROOM APARTMENT SURPRISINGLY EASY.

**Left:** SLIPCOVERS ARE TIMELESS IN THEIR APPEAL AND VERSATILITY, MAXIMIZING DESIGN OPTIONS AND ALLOWING A ROOM TO BE CHANGED SEASONALLY OR MORE OFTEN. THESE CRINKLED SLIPCOVERS VISIBLY SOFTEN A HARD-EDGED ROOM, AS DOES THE BEVY OF PILLOWS. THE COMBINATION OF SMOOTH, STRIPED, AND CRINKLED FABRICS ADDS TEXTURE TO THE MONOCHROMATIC PALETTE.

**Right:** Creamy white and peach-colored fabrics of various textures restore Old World glamour and tranquility to a Park Avenue bedroom built at the turn of the century. The room owes its sumptuous appearance to rich silks, which comprise the ornate canopy, soften the headboard, cover the eighteenth-century Adams window seat used here at the foot of the bed, and upholster the French Regency chair, whose lustrous silk moiré box pattern contrasts with the matte finish of the sofa and chaise lounge. **Above:** Upholstered in white matelassé (a patterned fabric distinguished by its raised woven designs), this lengthy chaise lounge is evocative of French Empire furnishings. Reminiscent details include the tufted cushion, gold feet, and hanging tassels. The sofa, another original by the same designer, features self welting and bullion fringe.

**Left:** Natural materials and animal hides, although not widely used today, were the first upholstery fabrics. This room, inspired by Austrian hunting lodges, appropriately includes leopard hides and dyed pigskins, which are particularly supple and comfortable. **Above:** The studied application of old fabrics and upholstery techniques reinstates a nineteenth-century spirit to this recently redecorated library. The embroidered ottoman with X-patterned banding and bullion fringe, tufted leather sofa, and drapes sewn from fabric with an authentic nineteenth-century pattern establish a quiet elegance.

**Above:** THE NUMEROUS PILLOWS FILLING THIS INDONESIAN-INSPIRED WOOD FRAME SOFA ARE MADE FROM EXCEPTIONALLY FINE NEEDLEPOINT. COMPLEMENTING THE DELICATE HANDIWORK AND TUCKED INTO THE ARMS OF THE SOFA ARE TWO ROLLED PILLOWS WITH HAND-BEADED TASSELS. **Right:** TWO NEEDLEPOINT PILLOWS DECORATE MOROCCAN-STYLE FURNITURE UPHOLSTERED IN LUXURIANT SUEDE WITH A BRAIDED SUEDE GALLOON TO CONCEAL NAIL HEADS. THE SUEDE, CHOSEN FOR ITS CONTEMPORARY LOOK, RELAXES AND UPDATES THE FORMAL EARLY NINETEENTH-CENTURY PIECES.

**Left:** Muted tones and soft fabrics distinguish sizable furniture without detracting from prominent Picasso murals. The sofa, actually a twin mattress and box spring, is covered in gaufrageed mohair-based velvet, a cut-pile fabric onto which a pattern has been burned. Batik-inspired hand-painted throw pillows of cotton and satin complement the artful feel of the room. **Above:** Hawaiian, Tahitian, and Indonesian textiles are mixed and matched to establish a languid mood in a 1950s California ranch home. Of particular interest are the eye-catching winged chair and sofa upholstered in a clever mix of raffia (a woven grass cloth) and other fabrics, introducing an unexpected layering of texture and color to the casual interior. A gray and white striped fabric on the club chair keeps the witty room from appearing too contrived.

**Right:** Upholstery tricks borrowed from techniques used to fashion Elizabethan costumes transform this once-upon-a-time formal dining room into a theatrical lounging area. The high-back chairs appear more like tailored suit jackets with peplum skirtings. The purplish metallic interlining is designed to look as though it was pulled through from the inside of the chair: Elizabethan clothing often included linings displayed as decoration. Two curved asymmetrical sofas are upholstered in red linen and playfully piped with green, gold, and red ball fringe, rounding out the whimsical scene.

**Above:** The layering of patterns, particularly geometric shapes, can add drama and richness to almost any room. Here, a simple diamond motif covers several surfaces in a 1930s–1940s "modernesque" Hollywood home. Patterned chairs are covered in hand-painted linen. **Right:** Through its harmony of pattern and color, this tiny guest room reveals how effectively upholstery can stir a mood. Here, a single dupioni silk print in a variety of colors focuses the eye on the bold use of color without lessening the impact of the spotted pattern.

**Right:** PEARLIZED CHARCOAL-GRAY LEATHER UPHOLSTERY COMPLEMENTS THE PHOTOGRAPHY COLLECTION IN THIS ROOM AND ACCENTS THE TRACES OF SILVER DUST IN THE CUSTOM-PLASTERED WALL TREATMENT. SELF WELTING GIVES BOTH CHAIR AND SOFA A FINISHED QUALITY AND HIGHLIGHTS THEIR DISTINCTIVE SHAPES. WHITE COTTON TAPESTRY PILLOWS WITH CONTRASTING WELTING COMPLETE THE CLASSIC TWO-TONE COLOR SCHEME. **Far right:** BLACK LEATHER UPHOLSTERY REVEALS ITS SEXY ATTITUDE ON A CONTEMPORARY BEDFRAME. IN THIS MINIMALLY DECORATED CAVERNOUS ROOM, DEEP TUFTING ON THE 15-FOOT (4.6M) HEADBOARD AND FOOTBOARD PROVIDES VISUAL INTEREST. CLASSIC BLACK AND WHITE STRIPES COVER THE CHAISE LOUNGE AND INFORMAL CUSHION OF THE REGENCY CHAIR.

MAASAI

**Left:** To instill a relaxed country feeling in a contemporary home, the designer of this living room tossed mohair and chenille throws and a Pendleton blanket over the couch. The interplay of plush textures and warm hues creates a symbolic nest—a place to bask in the abundant sunlight streaming through intentionally bare windows. Casual wicker chairs with pillows sewn from Mexican and Native American textiles provide additional seating. Tree stumps upholstered with needlepoint emphasize the country look.

**Left:** Mexican serapes and other ethnic textiles, traditionally used as blankets and clothing, bring color and credibility to restored western-style wood furniture. Designed as a tribute to cowboy Will Rogers, this room vividly illustrates the use of unconventional upholstery materials. **Right:** Like blankets, large pieces of fabric intended for other purposes can be enjoyed anew as stunning throws. Here, an eighteenth-century antique silk moiré curtain panel is set off by equally distinct pillows covered in tapestry and Venetian velvet.

**Above:** EACH ONE OF THESE INDIGO JACQUARD FABRICS WAS SPECIFICALLY DESIGNED TO EMPHASIZE THE SHAPE OF INDIVIDUAL PIECES OF FURNITURE. DIAMONDS, CAREFULLY SELECTED FOR THEIR ANGLE AND SIZE, ACCENTUATE THE GENEROUS PROPORTIONS OF THE COUCH AND SYMBOLICALLY REPRESENT ITS GRAND INSPIRATION—THE THREE DOMES OF SAN MARCO CATHEDRAL. THE MOVEMENT OF THE SQUIGGLE STRIPE ON THE HIGHLY STYLED CLUB CHAIRS EMPHASIZES THEIR CURVES, APPEARING TO SET THEM IN MOTION. THE DINING CHAIRS, WHICH SERVE AS ACCESSORIES AND ARE MOVED OFTEN, ARE COVERED IN A VERSATILE SOLID SILK. **Left:** THE INSPIRATION FOR THIS ROMANTIC TWO-TONE CHAIR CAME FROM A SPORTSWEAR COLLECTION. THE NOTICEABLE DISTINCTION BETWEEN THE ANTIQUE GOLD AND ANTIQUE SILVER FABRICS CHANGES THROUGHOUT THE DAY AS LIGHT CROSSES THE ROOM.

**Left:** Pale pink linen gives this Louis XVI–style carved pine chair, probably gilded at one time, an understated country elegance. The pale mint-green silk damask loosely draped over the small table balances the cloth-covered dining table beyond. **Below:** To make the most of a reproduction print fabric with a large repeat, the designer placed the carefully chosen angelic pattern on the back cushions of the white-painted bergère chairs.

**Above:** To emphasize furniture design or lineage, choose a basic pattern and fabric for the upholstered surfaces. Here, a simple black and white canvas stripe is all that is needed to distinguish a handsome Biedermeier chair. **Right:** Discovered at a flea market in Paris, this Gothic side chair was in fairly good repair—only the sides of the needlepoint cushion depicting a fox head were slightly frayed. To embellish it without lessening its romantic character, the designer simply added a French bullion fringe of complementary colors.

**Left:** DEEP PURPLE VELVET AND RICHLY COLORED FLORAL NEEDLEWORK SET APART THE DEMURE CHAUFFEUSE CHAIR FROM THE MORE HEAVILY UPHOLSTERED PIECES IN THIS ORNATE LIVING ROOM. **Below:** A MUTED FLORAL TAPESTRY FABRIC DISTINGUISHES THIS STATELY CARVED MAHOGANY ARMCHAIR IN A GENTLEMAN'S DRESSING ROOM PAINSTAKINGLY REFURBISHED TO ITS 1905–1910 GRANDEUR.

**Left:** Inspired by afternoon tea at a posh department store, this colorful cotton fabric pays homage to the teapot as an art form. The fun print features historically documented teapots from various schools, including majolica and Art Nouveau designs. Large patterns such as this one work best on equally large chairs.

**Right:** A rich crushed velvet, tufted on the back and seat cushions, gracefully accentuates the gentle curves of this upholstered armchair. The long box pleats of the front skirt are in keeping with the chair's classic lines and also prevent the short, round design from looking too stout.

**Right:** This lush bedroom—designed for a sophisticated teenager or young woman—tells the story of pattern on pattern and shows how small patterns can be successfully juxtaposed against larger ones. Cohesive color is especially important when blending patterns; by emphasizing similarity in hue, it underplays the differences in design. Placement is also relevant. Here, large prints are reserved for the most expansive surfaces, such as the bedding and curtains.

**Above, left:** Stripes contribute a tailored, modern look to a room blooming with floral prints. The lightly gathered skirt and braid trim impart a feminine quality to the chair.

**Above, right:** A deeply tufted 1930s English sofa is upholstered in a white cotton paisley decorated with a matching ball fringe. Colorful accent pillows dance across the top. The expanse of white noticeably opens up the heavily patterned room.

BALTHUS
RANSOME BOHEMIA IN LONDON
BERNERS FIRST CHILDHOOD AND FAR FROM THE

**Left:** INSIDE THIS CANVAS CABANA, THE METAL FRAMES OF ITALIAN FURNITURE ARE PURPOSEFULLY EXPOSED TO APPEAR LIGHT AND DELICATE. INDIAN COTTON, KNOWN FOR ITS DURABILITY AND COOLNESS, COVERS ALL UPHOLSTERED SURFACES. **Above:** TURQUOISE AND WHITE STRIPED TICKING ACCENTED BY GROSGRAIN RIBBON DRESSES DOWN AN ENGLISH MAHOGANY SETTEE. CUSHIONS FOR THE ORIGINAL NINETEENTH-CENTURY WICKER CHAIR WERE CUSTOM-MADE BY TRIMMING BORDERS FROM A COTTON CHINTZ, AND THEN STITCHING THEM TOGETHER WITH STRIPS OF WHITE BACKGROUND TAKEN FROM THE SAME FABRIC. THE TARTAN PLAID WAS ENLARGED TO SUIT A TEDDY ROOSEVELT–STYLE READING CHAIR.

**Left:** In needlepoint, widely used throughout the seventeenth century, a pattern or design is stitched onto canvas, unlike tapestry, where the image is actually created during the weaving. The center panel of this antique settee with tapestry upholstery is a fine needlepoint pattern of colored wools with silk edging.

**Left:** An unobtrusive, lightly striped slipcovered chair helps emphasize the exquisite tapestry and needlepoint fabrics covering an armchair, ottoman, and footrest. **Right:** A hearty cotton Belgian tapestry fabric was selected to make a new piece of furniture look old. The forest motif and rich colors work naturally with the deep wood frame of the Victorian-style sofa and still-life oil painting above.

**Right:** IN A ROOM DESIGNED FOR THE PRESENT, INFLUENCED BY THE PAST, AND LOOKING TO THE FUTURE, VARYING TEXTURES CREATE STRONG VISUAL INTEREST. FROM TIMELESS SILKS TO ENDURING WOOLS TO CLASSIC VELVETS, THE UPHOLSTERY COLLECTED HERE GIVES THIS TINY ONE-ROOM APARTMENT A UNIQUE PERSONALITY. **Above, left:** THE WINGED BACKS AND INSET CLOCKS OF THESE DINING CHAIRS PLAY ON THE NOTION OF TIME FLYING. NATURE, ANOTHER PREVALENT THEME, IS REPRESENTED BY THE MOSS-COLORED, STRIATED VELVET FABRIC, WHICH HAS A TEXTURE AND FEEL SIMILAR TO THE UNDERSIDE OF A LEAF. **Above, right:** SILK FLOWERS PUNCTUATE THE BOLSTER PILLOWS TUCKED INTO THE CURVED ARMS OF THE AMERICAN EMPIRE SOFA UPHOLSTERED IN A TEXTURED WOOL. LEAF DETAILS ON THE CUSTOM VELVET THROW CONTINUE THE NATURE THEME, AND ANTIQUE GOLD TRIM ADDS A TOUCH OF ELEGANCE.

**Below:** A straight skirt, sewn from cotton printed with faux marble geometric patterns, gives a boxy footrest an architectural look and softens the gray and white stripes of the chair. **Right:** Artistic upholstering reshaped an ordinary 1950s footrest into a plush ottoman befitting a regal aged leather wing chair. Ample stuffing, velvet fabric, decorative trim taken from an antique fabric, and bullion fringe—to conceal nondescript wood legs—performed the magic. An old woven Italian throw, a family heirloom, adds distinguished pattern and a truly personal touch to the grouping.

**Right:** Extremely versatile, ottomans make a design statement all their own. This button-topped tufted ottoman is dressed in red cotton damask. A Greek-key tape around the loose box pleat complements the classic gray and white cabana-striped chair fashioned in the ageless Directoire style. The entire ensemble is graphic and memorable, especially against the dark paneling.

**Left:** CHINTZ, FOREVER POPULAR IN DECORATING, IS A SHINY FINISH TYPICALLY APPLIED TO COTTON. IT WAS ORIGINALLY DEVELOPED TO MIMIC THE EXPENSIVE SILKS USED BY PRIVILEGED MEMBERS OF SOCIETY AT A PRICE THAT WAS AFFORDABLE TO THE MIDDLE CLASSES. USED EXTENSIVELY IN ONE CORNER OF THIS BEDROOM, CHINTZ PROVIDES A LIVELY BACKDROP FOR CONTRASTING COLORS AND TEXTURES, SUCH AS RUFFLED THROW PILLOWS, A SKIRTED DRESSING TABLE, AND VALANCE TRIMS.

**Left:** ASSORTED BLUE AND WHITE CHINTZ FABRICS WORK TOGETHER TO BRING FRENCH COUNTRY CHARM TO THIS URBAN BEDROOM. EQUALLY CALMING IS THE PRISTINE CANOPY, WHOSE LONG FLOWING WHITE CURTAINS AND FRINGED VALANCE SERVE AS A RESTING SPOT FOR THE EYE AS IT ROAMS ACROSS THE MANY PATTERNS.

**Right:** A PASSIONATE COLLECTOR OF EARLY TWENTIETH-CENTURY FURNITURE ACQUIRED THIS AUTHENTIC VIENNESE SOFA AND COMPANION ARMCHAIRS AND RESPECTFULLY RECOVERED THEM IN A FASHION BEFITTING THEIR HERITAGE. SUEDE PIGSKIN RETURNS THE PIECES TO THEIR ORIGINAL STATURE.

**Above and right:** LEATHER IS ESPECIALLY LUXURIOUS WHEN USED MONOCHROMATICALLY ON SEVERAL PIECES IN THE SAME ROOM. UPHOLSTERING EACH PIECE IN THE SAME COLOR AND GRADE OF LEATHER FOCUSES ATTENTION ON THE CONTEMPORARY FURNITURE IN THESE ROOMS RATHER THAN ON THE COVERINGS.

**Left:** Silk taffetas, praised for their intense luster, imbue this Moroccan-inspired dining room with exotic elegance. Metal chairs evocative of Indian and Egyptian interiors are made more expressive with different-colored seat cushions. Individual fabrics were sewn together in diamond patterns to cover the fireplace stool, camel stool, and stand-alone chair, cleverly adding another layer of silken opulence to the dramatic space. **Above:** The Mobix chair, composed of metal and an upholstered button-shaped seat, underscores the impact of a bright burst of color on even the simplest furniture designs.

**Above:** SILK AND COTTON TAFFETAS IN JUBILANT SPRINGTIME PASTELS ENHANCE THE SHAPELY FURNITURE IN THIS PENTHOUSE APARTMENT. THE EXAGGERATED WROUGHT IRON FRAMES APPEAR CARTOONLIKE AGAINST THE THICK UPHOLSTERED CUSHIONS. **Right:** THE FULLY UPHOLSTERED PIECES IN THE ADJACENT ROOM FOLLOW THE SAME LINES AS THE WROUGHT-IRON FRAMES. HAND-PAINTED COTTON SATIN PILLOWS PICK UP THE COLORS OF THE CUSTOM FLORAL MURAL AND MATCHING WALL HANGING.

MATISSE IN MOROCCO
MATISSE IN MOROCCO
HORST

VEGAS

**Below:** The striped fabric chosen for the sofa also covers a nineteenth century–style ottoman. Multicolored moss trim adds just a hint of Victoriana to the updated piece.

**Above:** In a seaside summer house, crisp cotton fabrics in cool shades provide a relaxed tone and refreshing feeling. The collection is a mix of found pieces and family heirlooms. **Left:** Nineteenth-century English chairs, reupholstered to complement the striped sofa, maintain the casual ambience of the living room.

LA COTE D'AZUR
THE LANDMARKS OF NEW YORK

**Left:** THE WONDERFUL LUSTER OF LINEN DENIM SOFTENS THE LINES OF THESE OVERSCALED ARMCHAIRS. THE FABRIC, OBTAINED FROM A CLOTHING MANUFACTURER, IS NOT OVERLY DRESSY OR FUSSY IN APPEARANCE, BUT IS DISTINGUISHED BY ITS UNUSUAL WEAVE AND TEXTURE. THE TURN-OF-THE-CENTURY CHINESE SILKS COVERING THE ACCENT PILLOWS REMAIN COOL TO THE TOUCH AND STAND OUT AGAINST THE PALE PALETTE.

**Left:** USED JUDICIOUSLY, LARGE-SCALE GRAPHIC PRINTS CAN TRANSFORM NONDESCRIPT FURNITURE INTO SHOWCASE PIECES, ESPECIALLY WHEN PLACED NEAR SUBDUED SOLIDS REVEALING ONLY A HINT OF TEXTURE. **Right:** SOMETIMES THE BEST REASON TO CHOOSE A FABRIC IS PERSONAL. THE DESIGNER AND OWNER OF THIS HOME, WHO HAS ALWAYS BEEN FOND OF SCENIC TOILE DE JOUY, SELECTED AN ANIMAL MOTIF TO COMPLEMENT HER HOME, A RENOVATED COUNTRY BARN. A SMATTERING OF OTHER BLACK AND WHITE PATTERNS GIVES THE INTIMATE GROUPING A COMFORTABLE, CASUAL FLAIR.

**Above:** THE SILK DAMASK COVERING THIS PERIOD SETTEE IS A REPRODUCTION FABRIC HISTORICALLY APPROPRIATE TO THE DESIGN OF THE WOOD FRAME. IT WAS CHOSEN SPECIFICALLY TO BLEND WITH THE OMBRÉ-PATTERNED WALLPAPER, ITSELF REPRODUCED FROM AN AUTHENTIC 1830S DESIGN. **Right:** IN THIS ROOM, THE MATCH OF FABRIC TO WALLPAPER HAPPENED BY CHANCE; THE DESIGNER COINCIDENTALLY OWNED A SILK DAMASK THAT BORE A STRIKING SIMILARITY TO THE EXISTING WALLPAPER. ADJACENT TO SILK DRAPES AND HIGHLIGHTED BY A NINETEENTH-CENTURY VENETIAN CHANDELIER, THE TWIN PATTERNS APPEAR HARMONIOUS AND ELEGANT.

Who's Who
in
Interior Design

**Far left:** An original—and complete—nineteenth-century neoclassical Italian salon set takes command of this richly appointed living room. The striped blue silk fabric—also original—gracefully emphasizes the lines and curves of the ornate and rare pieces. **Left:** The only new piece in this neoclassical salon, the couch is covered in a very fine gold-colored linen velvet outlined with a narrow band of trim.

**Left:** Warm colors and comfortable textures make this fireplace grouping appear especially cozy. The sofa is covered in a nude leather, selected for its sensual feel; the linen velvet chairs were also chosen for their luxurious texture. **Above:** The channeled Thailand silk throw gracing the back of this sleeper sofa actually changes color with the light, metamorphosing from "greige" (gray-beige) to dusty rose. It also serves as a wrap on cool evenings. Richly colored velvet and silk pillows sparkle like jewels against the sofa's neutral tones.

**Right:** AN ENGLISH COTTON FLORAL PRINT LENDS A ROMANTIC AIR TO A HIGH-BACKED QUEEN ANNE SETTEE AND INSPIRES THE CHOICE OF COLORS AND FABRICS ELSEWHERE IN THE ROOM, INCLUDING THE RUG AND THE MULTICOLORED SILK FRINGE OF THE LAMBREQUIN.

**Right:** THE DARK PANELING ENCASING THIS TUDOR-INSPIRED LIVING ROOM BEGGED FOR LIGHT-COLORED UPHOLSTERY TO OPEN UP THE SPACE. CHAIRS COVERED IN RED FRENCH SILK DAMASK SHOW THE ENGLISH INFLUENCES OF VICTORIAN TUFTING AND AN INVERTED KICK-PLEAT SKIRT. BULLION FRINGE ON THE MATELASSÉ SOFA IS ALSO VICTORIAN, AS IS THE ECLECTIC COLLECTION OF ANTIQUE THROW PILLOWS, WHICH ENLIVENS THE SOFT COLOR SCHEME.

# Sources

**Architects and Interior Designers**

Pages 6, 29
Ron Meyers
Los Angeles, CA
(213) 851-7576

Page 7
Van-Martin Rowe
Pasadena, CA
(818) 577-4736

Pages 8, 36 (right)
Dennis Rolland
New York, NY
(212) 644-0537

Page 9
Pauline Boardman, Ltd.
New York, NY
(212) 288-8379

Page 10
Thad Hayes Design, Inc.
New York, NY
(212) 571-1234

Page 11
Billy W. Francis
Design Decoration, Inc.
New York, NY
(212) 734-3588

Page 12
Mark Zeff Consulting Group, Inc.
New York, NY
(212) 580-7090

Page 13
Sandra Nunnerley, Inc.
New York, NY
(212) 472-9341

Pages 14–15
Clare Fraser, Designer
New York, NY
(212) 737-3479

Page 16
Hutton Wilkinson
Los Angeles, CA
(213) 874-7760

Page 18
Lori Ward
Use-What-You-Have Interiors
New York, NY
(212) 288-8888

Page 19 (top and bottom)
Vincent Wolf Associates, Inc.
New York, NY
(212) 465-0590

Pages 20–21, 37 (left)
Noel Jeffrey, Inc.
New York, NY
(212) 935-7775

Page 22
Tony Duquete
Los Angeles, CA
(310) 271-3574

Page 23
David Easton
New York, NY
(212) 486-6704

Page 24
Linda Garland for Nancy Corzine Showrooms
Los Angeles, CA
(310) 652-4859

Pages 25, 64–65
Robert Metzger Interiors, Inc.
New York, NY
(212) 371-9800

Pages 26, 56–57
Greg Jordan
New York, NY
(212) 421-1474

Page 27
Jarrett Hedborg Interior Design
Sherman Oaks, California
(818) 501-4239
painting by Harry Carmean
Los Angeles, CA
(213) 654-2237

Page 28 (top)
Charles Riley, Designer
Los Angeles, CA
(213) 383-5838
New York, NY
(212) 473-4173

Page 28 (bottom)
Gregory Evans
Los Angeles, CA
(213) 250-7014

Pages 30, 31, 49
Fox-Nahem Design
New York, NY
(212) 929-1485

Page 33 (top)
Van-Martin Rowe
Pasadena, CA
(818) 577-4736
screen by Annie Kelly, Designer
Los Angeles, CA
(213) 876-8030
broken tile ball by Van-Martin Rowe
stools by the late John Haymer

Page 33 (bottom)
Stephen Miller Siegel, Architect
New York, NY
(212) 460-0541

Pages 34–35
Donghia Furniture/Textiles
Furniture by John Hutton
New York, NY
(212) 925-2777
London, England
(071) 823-3456

Page 36 (left)
Jacquelynne P. Lanham Design
Atlanta, GA
(404) 364-0472

Page 37 (right)
Thomas M. Beeton, Inc. Interior Decoration
Beverly Hills, CA
(310) 247-0325

Page 38 (left)
John Robert Moore II

Page 38 (right)
Natural Park Service
Sagamore Hill National Historic Society
Oyster Bay, NY
(516) 922-4788

Page 39 (left)
Pierre Frey
New York, NY
(212) 355-7200

Pages 40–41, 50–51
Mario Buatta
New York, NY
(212) 988-6811

Page 42
Jeff Bilhuber, Inc.
New York, NY
(212) 517-7673

Page 43
Anthony Buratta, William Diamond
William Diamond Design
New York, NY
(212) 966-8892

Page 44
Mark Hampton
New York, NY
(212) 753-4110

Page 45 (left)
Tryon Palace Historic Sites and Gardens
Bern, NC
(919) 638-1560

Page 45 (right)
Drew Atherton
Brookline, MA
(617) 566-7602

Pages 46–47
Victoria Hagan Interiors
New York, NY
(212) 472-1290

Page 48 (left)
Lorraine Henry
Larchmont, NY
(800) 332-7840

Page 53
furniture by the late Josef Hofman

Page 54
George Constant, Inc.
New York, NY
(212) 751-1907

Page 55
Monique and Sergio Savarese for Dialogica
Los Angeles, CA
(213) 951-1993
New York, NY
(212) 966-1934

Pages 58–59
Carolyn Guttilla/Plaza One
Locust Valley, NY
(516) 671-9280

Page 60
Cary McCabe
McBride & McCabe Interiors
McBride & Associates, Architects
New York, NY
(212) 941-0818

Page 61 (left)
Aero Studio
New York, NY
(212) 966-4700

Page 61 (right)
C.K. Design
Los Angeles, CA
(310) 476-1824

Page 62
The Gracey Mansion Conservancy
New York, NY
(212) 570-0985
settee owned by the Museum of the City of New York

Page 63
Annie Kelly, Designer
Los Angeles, CA
(213) 876-8030

Pages 66, 67
John F. Saladino, Inc.
New York, NY
(212) 752-2440

Pages 68–69
Richard L. Ridge
New York, NY
(212) 472-0608

**PHOTOGRAPHY CREDITS**

Feliciano: 39 (left), 52 (bottom)

Courtesy of Tom Fox/Fox-Nahem Design: 30 (Pieter Estersohn), 31 (Lynn Reynolds), 49 (Lynn Reynolds)

Tria Giovan: 18, 52 (top)

Mick Hales: 9, 36 (left), 38 (left), 62

Lizzie Himmel: 42, 44, 67

image/dennis krukowski: 23, 25, 38 (right)

Michael Mundy: 10, 12, 13, 19 (top), 26, 33 (bottom), 34, 35, 37 (left), 43, 48 (right), 55, 56, 57, 60, 61 (left), 66

David Phelps: 48 (left)

Tim Street-Porter: 6, 7, 16, 17, 22, 24, 27, 28 (both), 29, 32, 33 (top), 37 (right), 61 (right), 63

Paul Rocheleau: 45 (left)

Courtesy of Dennis Rolland/Dennis Rolland, Inc.: 8 (Michael Mundy), 36 (right) (Michael Mundy)

Eric Roth: 45 (right), 53

Peter Vitale: 2, 11, 14, 15 (both), 19 (bottom), 20, 21, 39 (right), 40 (both), 41, 46 (both), 47, 50, 51, 54, 58, 59 (both), 64, 65, 68, 69

# INDEX